Winston Churchill

The Life, Lessons & Rules For Success

Jack Morris

□

Table of Contents

Introduction

From schoolboy failure to wartime hero, Winston Churchill had an astonishing life ensuring his place in history. It is no secret Churchill had a passion for war, as a young officer he served in British India, the Anglo Sudan War and the Second Boer War. From being captured as a prisoner of war whilst in Africa, he escaped to safety becoming a minor national hero in the process. From relative failure through his role in World War I to commanding Great Britain out of their darkest hour and eventually onto victory during World War II, there can be no doubt of the tenacity shown by the man during what can only be described as an extremely eventful and interesting life. On the frontline of politics for more than 50 years, Churchill held a variety of political and cabinet positions. Serving as Prime Minister on two separate occasions, his radio broadcasts and speeches were instrumental in inspiring the British Resistance during the difficult times of 1940-41 when the British Empire stood almost alone in resisting Hitler's Nazi Germany. It is quite easy to see why in a 2002 poll; Sir Winston Leonard Spencer-Churchill was named the 'Greatest Briton' of all time.

Chapter 1: Family and Early Life

As an adult, he collected all kinds of titles from the military, from the government, and from his grateful countrymen – but as a child, he was just Winston Leonard, born on November 30, 1874, the first son of Lord Randolph Churchill and Jeanette "Jennie" Jerome. He was born in a suite of rooms contained within the heart of Blenheim Palace, the great country house and principal residence of the Dukes of Marlborough.

Wealth, power, and privilege surrounded Winston practically from the moment that he was born. His father, Lord Randolph, was the third-born son of the 7th Duke of Marlborough, who by the time of his first son's birth had become a by-name in British politics through his promotion of the ideals of progressive Conservatism. He felt that the Tories should support and promulgate popular reforms instead of opposing them, and he used his charisma and his talent for making speeches to promote that agenda throughout his political career.

Although Lord Randolph was not on the track to inherit his family's noble titles, he could still partake of the immense prestige and respect accorded them. It could be said that he belonged to a high-born family indeed; well before Winston was born, the Dukes of Marlborough – whose very line had begun with John Churchill, one of the first generals of the British Army – had married into the equally noble and esteemed Spencer family, meaning that their descendants could take the formidable double-barreled surname of Spencer-Churchill. However, for simplicity's sake, Lord Randolph, and his sons after him, were all referred to by the last name of "Churchill" throughout their lives.

His mother, Jennie, was similarly born with a silver spoon in her mouth. She was the eldest daughter of the New York stock-market speculator, yachtsman, horse-race aficionado, and financier Leonard Jerome. In the eyes of American society at that time, that placed her on an equal footing with the hereditary noble families of Europe. The family's immense wealth allowed her and her sisters to become well-known socialites on the other side of the Atlantic Ocean. She had been introduced to Lord Randolph Churchill by no less than the future king Edward VII, and was well-known for her wit and beauty.

Winston spent part of his childhood in Dublin; at the time, his paternal grandfather, the 7th Duke of Marlborough, was serving as the Viceroy of Ireland, and had taken his son (Winston's father) on as his private secretary. Some historians and biographers have since claimed that Winston's interest in military matters may have had its roots in the many parades and ceremonies that would take place around the Viceroy's residence.

It was the common practice among the middle and upper classes at the time for the parents to have little to no hand in their children's upbringing, and Winston's parents did not see fit to deviate from that practice. In Dublin, it was a governess, not his parents, who taught him the traditional three R's (reading, writing, and 'rithmetic). His emotions and childhood interests, too, were spent with someone who wasn't connected to the family by blood ties: his nanny, Elizabeth Ann Everest. She became a permanent presence in young Winston's life practically from the cradle, and in return he regarded her as a substitute for his emotionally distant mother. She was his caretaker and confidant, and he addressed her by the affectionate title of "Woom", or "Woomany".

Winston's younger brother, John, was born during the family's sojourn in Dublin. He seemed to have been a loving and good-natured younger brother, who did better than Winston ever did at school. Lord Randolph and, on occasion, Jennie, would write letters to Winston in which they pleaded with him to apply himself to his schoolwork as his brother did.

Winston chose to be ruled by his independent and rebellious nature through his school years. Though he was possessed of an innate talent and a keen interest in both mathematics and history, he was not interested in studying the classics, making his teachers at St. George's, Brunswick, and Harrow despair of him. And he seemed to feel the same way about them: particularly when he was at Harrow, he would write long letters to his mother, begging her to allow him to leave school and go home, or at the very least to come and visit him. Her silence in that regard may have contributed to his sense of being left adrift, and may have contributed to the fact that he remained at the bottom of the class throughout his school years.

One of the few bright spots in that period of Winston's life was his stint in the Harrow Rifle Corps. This program still exists today, under the aegis of the Combined Cadet Force. In Winston's time, the members of the corps, or cadets, were taught drills and marksmanship, and – then as now – were encouraged to consider going on to become officers in the armed forces.

During the school holidays, Winston would rejoin his parents and brother either at home or at the various estates of other family members and close friends. On one such occasion when he was 18, that estate, belonging to his aunt Lady Wimborne, was located in Bournemouth. Later on in life, he described it as forty to fifty acres of forest that abruptly terminated in cliffs overlooking the English Channel. Rustic bridges crossed the many cracks and canyons, and they were a venue for the many boys' games that Winston, his brother John, and their cousins would play.

However, it was one of those bridges that nearly ended Winston's life before he could become a political powerhouse. With his playmates chasing him, he ran out onto a bridge overlooking pine trees, where they cornered him at both ends. Rather than be tagged or captured, he chose to jump over the railings, intending to be caught in one of the trees so that he could slide down the trunk and get back to safe ground.

He missed the trees, and fell to the hard ground beneath the bridge – a fall that he later estimated at about 29 feet.

It took him three days to regain consciousness, and a further three months before he could get out of bed and walk on his own again.

The next great crisis in his life struck within the next three years. His father's health had been in decline all throughout the 1890s, and neither the exhilaration of winning horse races nor the various trips he made to sunnier and more congenial destinations around the world could stop him from getting weaker and frailer with each passing day. By Christmas of 1894 it was clear that he would no longer rise from his sickbed. Lord Randolph's premature death at the age of 45 convinced Winston, then about 21, that he would also die young – and that therefore he should make the most of what he felt was his limited time, and quickly become a significant person in his own right.

Many claims have been made about the relationship that Winston had with his father: chief among them being that Lord Randolph never cared for him, or that Lord Randolph believed that Winston and his brother had been fathered by other men. However, both Winston and John eagerly exchanged letters with their father, and Lord Randolph made it clear that he regarded the two of them as his actual sons and heirs – not just to Winston and John, but to his friends and close correspondents as well. In return, Winston eventually came to believe that it was his task to follow his father into politics.

But Winston's other conviction that he, too, was destined for an early grave could only have been strengthened when his beloved "Woom", Mrs. Everest, died a few months after his father did. The family had abruptly let her go after her long years of devoted service, forcing her to take shelter with her sister in North London. As soon as he learned that she was gravely ill, he rushed to her side, and then their roles were reversed for a short time as he helped to make her more comfortable. Winston paid for her funeral and the tombstone that marked her grave, and went so far as to ask the clergyman who had been Mrs. Everest's previous employer to perform the burial rites.

Chapter 2: Military Service

By the time Winston left school in 1893, his early interest in military matters could only have been further stoked by both his stint in the Harrow Rifle Corps, and the knowledge that his ancestors had won great renown and honor as soldiers and officers. For him, the logical next step would be to enter the armed forces – and that was how he found himself applying to enter the Royal Military College at Sandhurst. At the time, the RMC graduated infantry and cavalry officers, who would then be commissioned into either the British or the Indian army. He faced severe difficulties right at the outset of his military career, however; he failed the RMC entrance examination twice, and only got through on the third attempt. In addition, he applied to become part of the cavalry officer class because the grade required for entrance into that group was lower than that needed to be part of the infantry officer class. And even though he had shown a talent for mathematics at Harrow, he disliked the idea of having to take further classes in that subject, something that was part of the infantry officer class's curriculum.

Cavalry strategy and tactics seemed to be more his speed, and he seemed to do much better at the RMC compared to his time at Harrow, graduating near the top of his class. This gave him the opportunity to transfer to an infantry regiment – but even though he knew that the transfer would have made his father happy, he chose to remain a cavalry officer.

The year 1895 was a bittersweet one for Winston, as he began it in mourning for the death of his father, and then entered the British armed forces with the rank of cornet, or second lieutenant, becoming part of the 4th Queen's Own Hussars – one of the units that had won fame in the ill-fated Charge of the Light Brigade, which took place during the Crimean War. From there, he proceeded to his first posting, as an observer during the Cuban War of Independence – but was soon obliged to rush back to Britain when he received the news of his nanny's terminal illness. The posting to Cuba meant that Winston would have his first opportunity to travel to the United States, where his mother had been born; he sailed from Liverpool to New York, and would go on from there to Florida, and thence to the port of Havana, which was still a Spanish stronghold against the Cuban insurgents. Though he was only in New York for a shirt time, he still found an opportunity to be introduced to the American politician Bourke Cockran. The Irish-American Cochran's approach to oratory became a great influence on Winston, as did his obvious love for and appreciation of his own country's beliefs. This was an important influence on the young Winston, who soon after this meeting began to develop a love for America.Also with Winston at this time was fellow officer Reginald Barnes; together, the two of them were tasked to compile reports and observations on the Spanish Army's strategies, and on the guerrilla warfare tactics that were being employed by the insurgent Cubans. While traveling with units of Spanish soldiers, Winston and Reginald saw at first hand the rebels' various methods of frustrating their enemies' efforts. Though there was an existing network of train tracks to connect the various Spanish fortifications, the rebels' skill at derailing the trains meant that the young British observers had to endure the difficulties of rerouted trips and innumerable delays. This gave Winston plenty of time to take notes on the effects of the conflict. He saw the burned houses and the broken fences at first hand, and from time to time he would also catch sight of men on horses who were spying on the Spanish forces on behalf of the insurgence.

Winston came under fire for the first time in his life on his twenty-first birthday, when he mounted up with the Spanish troops in order to find and engage a rebel camp.

At the same time, Winston and Reginald were caught up in the tangled webs of intelligence and counter-intelligence – because while they had been legitimately sent to Cuba to observe the Spanish Army's movements, they also had another set of orders to follow, this one coming from the then-Director of British Military Intelligence, Edward Chapman. He asked them to collect information on the weapons that the Spanish Army had brought to the conflict, so that the United Kingdom would have up-to-date information on another country's military strength.

In short, they were observers, but they were also spies, watching both sides of the war and sending home whatever useful information they could find.

The Cuban sojourn lasted for just a few weeks, but it was more than enough time for Winston to understand the difference between studying history and observing it at first hand. In this case, he became convinced that there was no way that the Spanish Army would ever gain the upper hand in the conflict, since they were kept on the defensive by the rebels' superior tactics. He felt that those tactics were enabled by the local populace: after all, the rebels came from among them, and were, on the surface, fighting the hated Spanish on their behalf.

While most of his sympathies lay with the Cubans who wanted to gain their freedom, he also feared the overall strategy that they had chosen: that of revolt. He wanted the rebels to win their freedom, but he feared the consequences of that victory: he feared that racial violence and further conflict would follow, perpetuating a vicious cycle of violence that would leave no room for actual independence or prosperity to take hold.

He brought a few odd habits home from Cuba, at the end of his brief posting: a taste for rum cocktails, and for the item that would become an essential and indelible part of his public image for the rest of his life – a good Havana cigar. He became such an aficionado that a specific size of cigar was eventually named for him; in cigar parlance, a Churchill is in the shape of a cylinder with straight sides, has one open end and one closed end, and measures exactly seven inches long. As an officer, Winston received the salary that was his due, as well as an allowance from his mother – but he continued to feel that he did not have enough money to support the lifestyle that most of his brother officers did, so he needed to look for ways to supplement his income. At the same time, he was also thinking about his future prospects: in particular, he was keen on catching the attention of the British public, since he would need their favorable regard in order to launch a career in politics. So he parlayed his family's influence, his mother's network of connections, his considerable interest in history, and his fledgling skill as a writer into becoming a war correspondent. His dispatches from the Cuban jungle to the

London Daily Graphic were packed full of evocative details and terse descriptions of combat, sabotage, and precarious escapes from rebel forces, and soon won him public acclaim, as well as additional income. These articles, which were among his first works to be published, marked Winston out as a writer to watch out for, and not just in journalistic circles. On receiving his next assignment, Winston packed his bags and headed for India, which was still a steadfast and loyal part of the British Empire at that time. Bangalore was far removed from any conflict, and there were few duties for Winston to take part in, aside from his regiment's regular polo matches. He needed something to stave off the boredom, and at the same time to while away the hot and humid afternoons, so he wrote letters to family and friends – and began to pay even closer attention to the politics of his home country. In particular, he detailed his political opinions to his mother, and asked her to send him copies of the Parliamentary debates – not just those of the present, but also from previous generations.

In return, he took her advice to improve his mind by reading –
and he added the great historical works of the day to the
classics that he had detested in school, but now had a chance
to read at his own pace. Gibbons's Decline and Fall of the
Roman Empire, Macaulay's History of England, and Plato's
Republic became his companions, as did Reade's The
Martyrdom of Man. Though the thought of obtaining a degree
in history, politics, or economics crossed his mind, he did not
know enough Latin and Greek to get into the universities of
the time.

Even as he made great strides in the area of self-improvement,
Winston continued to keep an eye out for the various conflicts
playing out all over the world. When he heard about the
Greco-Turkish war in 1897, he attempted to travel to that part
of the world in order to report on it – and to fight, if needed.
However, that war came to an abrupt halt while he was still en
route to Turkey, so he went on to London instead. He arrived
just prior to the beginning of the social season, which meant
that he was on home soil for a once-in-a-lifetime event: the
Diamond Jubilee of Queen Victoria.

He then made his way to the North-West Frontier of British India (now part of Pakistan), where he soon found himself on the front lines of what would become the First Mohmand Campaign. This time, even as he participated as an active officer, he was also serving as a war correspondent for the Daily Telegraph and the Allahabad Pioneer. He sent home various reports on the fight between the British brigades and the various Pashtun tribes in the area.

Winston quickly took note of the similarities between this conflict and the Cuban War of Independence: the Pashtun tribes had the advantage of knowing how to move and how to fight in the inhospitable terrain of the Malakand District and its surrounding areas, just as the Cuban insurgents seemed to know the island's jungles by heart. More importantly, the Pashtun tribes nearly instinctively resorted to the hit-and-run tactics that had become familiar to Winston during his time in Cuba. However, this time it was the British army that carried the day, thanks to their superior weapons, strategies, and intelligence.

Winston used his news articles and the rest of his observations and experiences during this conflict as the basis for his first non-fiction book, The Story of the Malakand Field Force.

On returning to Bangalore from the Malakand district, he tried his hand at writing a novel, producing what would become his only major fictional work. Savrola was, on the surface, a Victorian romance set in a fictional European country, but for Winston it was also a recapitulation of his thoughts and experiences in Cuba. It was first serialized in Macmillan's Magazine, and was then published in book form two years later, receiving mixed reviews.

Winston was transferred to Egypt in 1898, and joined the 21st Lancers who were fighting in the Mahdist War; notably, he took part in the penultimate battle at Omdurman. The Lancers' charge became known as the last meaningful British charge of cavalry; Winston wrote about it in his dispatches to the Morning Post and in his book The River War: An Account of the Reconquest of the Soudan (sic). The charge was also immortalized in several paintings.

After the Lancers were pulled back and given fresh orders, Winston returned to England to complete his interrupted leave, then made his way back to India. To his dismay, this was where he found out about a new rule that the British Army had promulgated, which prohibited officers on active duty from also being war correspondents. That led him to tender his resignation in May of 1899.

Despite his disillusionment with the regular army, he was still keen on serving in the armed forces; to this end, he joined the Imperial Yeomanry in 1902, becoming a Captain of the Queen's Own Oxfordshire Hussars – and ultimately following in the footsteps of his own ancestors, as the Churchill family had been instrumental in the regiment's formation. He was eventually promoted to Major, gaining command of one of the regiment's squadrons.

Winston remained in his post until 1916, when he transferred to the officer corps of the territorial reserves; he retired from the latter at the age of fifty.

Chapter 3: Marriage and Children

Having become somewhat of a civilian by the turn of the 20th century, Winston returned to England in order to enter public life and politics. He had participated in the 1899 Oldham by-election, standing with James Mawdsley as the Conservative Party's candidates for the borough's seats in Parliament. However, the rival Liberal Party took both seats.

Winston then went to South Africa to report on the Second Boer War for the Morning Post. He was captured by the Boers as he was traveling with a scouting expedition, and was interned in Pretoria – then shot to prominence in Britain by staging a daring and successful escape to Portuguese East Africa (now Mozambique). He was given an opportunity to go home, but he declined it in favor of a commission offered by the South African Light Horse, who were marching in order to capture Pretoria. He crossed paths with his cousin the Duke of Marlborough during this conflict, and together they forced a large contingent of Boer prison guards to surrender.

He followed that up with a triumphant entrance into politics during the 1900 general election, where he was finally able to win one of the two Oldham seats in Parliament. He then embarked on a lecture tour, visiting cities across both Britain and the United States and creating a name for himself in the world at large.

Winston first met his future wife, Clementine Ogilvy Hozier, in 1904, at a ball hosted by the Liberal politician the Earl of Crewe – but it was not until 1908 that romance blossomed between them. He was entranced not just by her good looks but also by her intelligence and distinct character. Their courtship was brief, as was their engagement; they were married that same year.

Clementine was the daughter of Lady Blanche Hozier; there is much debate as to her biological father. Her legal father, Henry Montague Hozier, was reputed to be sterile; moreover, her parents were both guilty of infidelity, having each taken different lovers. Historians point to either William George "Bay" Middleton or Algernon Bertram Freeman-Mitford as the most likely candidates – but Winston ignored all of the potential scandal in favor of Clementine herself.

While history remembers her as a loyal, loving, and supportive wife to Winston, Clementine was also capable of doing great things all by herself. She was active on the home front during the world wars, working on behalf of munitions workers during the First World War, and with the Red Cross during the Second. She was made a Commander of the Order of the British Empire in 1918; that rank was then upgraded to Dame Grand Cross in 1946.

The Churchills would end up having five children in all: Diana, born in 1909; Randolph, born in 1911; Sarah, born in 1914; Marigold, born in 1918; and Mary, born in 1922.

After spending several terms at the Royal Academy of Dramatic Art, Diana followed in her father's footsteps and joined the Wrens (Women's Royal Naval Service) during the Second World War. However, she committed suicide with an overdose of barbiturates in 1963, after suffering multiple nervous breakdowns over the course of her life.

Randolph started out in his professional life as a journalist, then switched gears to stand for Parliament, in much the same way as his father and grandfather before him. But he did not meet with success on the political track, only succeeding in taking a seat in the House of Commons in WWII. He was also hampered by a dependence on alcohol and an abrasive personality, both of which would earn him many enemies.

It was in the field of literature that Randolph found his calling. Having inherited Winston's skill with the English language, he did well as a gossip columnist, and was entrusted with the job of editing his father's speeches for publication. He published a memoir of his early life, entitled Twenty-One Years, and started work on an official biography of his father Winston, completing two volumes before his death.

Using the assumed last name of "Oliver", Sarah also joined the British armed forces during the Second World War, signing up with the Women's Auxiliary Air Force to work in photo reconnaissance. After the war, she became an actress and dancer, appearing both on stage and in movies such as Royal Wedding, starring opposite Fred Astaire. She also showed off her talents in the field of visual art with a series of prints depicting Winston and his great drive and ambition; the series included a drawing that she had done of him.

Like her brother, she struggled with alcoholism; she was arrested several times for creating a scene on the street while drunk, and spent a short period of time in HM Prison Holloway. It is thought that her drinking problems contributed to her death.

Marigold died just before she was to turn three years old. She was placed in the care of a governess named Mademoiselle Rose, who near the beginning of August, 1921, reported to Clementine and Winston that Marigold had caught a cold, but seemed to have made a complete recovery. Unknown to everyone else, however, the cold turned into something worse: septicemia (now referred to as sepsis). Marigold died on the 23rd of August of that year.Mary was active on the home front during the Second World War; like her mother, she served with the Red Cross, and additionally with the Women's Voluntary Service. She also joined the Auxiliary Territorial Service, which was the women's branch of the British Army at the time, working on anti-aircraft batteries. Eventually she rose to the rank of Junior Commander in that service. In addition, she would accompany Winston on some of his overseas trips, serving as one of his aides-de-camp.

After the war, Mary went on to work with various public and non-government organizations, and also became a successful author. Most of her books have to do with her immediate family, although she also wrote about one of the earlier Dukes of Marlborough. She wrote and published an official biography of her mother Clementine, which won popular and critical acclaim; she also edited and published a selection of her parents' letters, to which she added information that would help place their statements in the correct historical, personal, and familial contexts. She published her own memoirs in 2012.

For her work with humanitarian organizations, Mary was made a Dame Commander of the Order of the British Empire; she was also made a Lady Companion of the Order of the Garter. She died in 2014, having been the only one of her siblings to live into her nineties.

Chapter 4: Before the World Wars

Despite entering politics as a staunch Conservative, over the next few years Winston found it more and more difficult to align his political opinions with those held by the leaders of his party. Initially, he disagreed with fellow Conservative politican St John Broderick, then sitting as the Secretary of State for War, who proposed that the British army be expanded to six corps, with the three new groups to be granted the power to form an expeditionary force that would be sent to various destinations overseas. The speech to oppose that proposal was meticulously planned over six weeks, and Winston delivered it with rhetorical flourish and grace, speaking for over an hour without needing to check any notes. He also made speeches opposing trade protectionism; instead, he advocated free trade – a stance that he retained nearly all throughout his public and political life. Unfortunately, the Parliamentary borough of Oldham supported the imposition of tariffs on cheap foreign textiles, in order to protect the home-grown cotton-spinning firms. He was effectively disowned by the Oldham voters as a result of his advocacy. In 1904 he switched his party allegiance from the Conservatives to the Liberals. This eventually opened the door for him to rise to a position in the Cabinet, becoming President of the Board of Trade – which position he used to help open the door for the series of legislative acts known as the Liberal welfare reforms (1906-1914). These laws sought to include the quality of life for children, the elderly, the sick, and various groups of workers: miners, sailors, farmers, and shop workers. Legislation was introduced to bring down unemployment through public works such as a ship-building program, as well as the labor exchanges, where employers could post job vacancies and would-be employees could look for work.

Winston and his fellow Liberals also worked on the passage of "the People's Budget", which would impose new taxes on the wealthy for the purpose of funding various social welfare programs for the poor. This resulted in fierce fighting between the various political parties of the time – and Winston threw himself straight into the thick of things, delivering speeches to gather support among various constituencies. These speeches became even more effective over time as he learned how to add various kinds of humor depending on who was listening, ranging from dry wit to broad jokes that nevertheless made the listeners pause to think about his words.

With the arguments over the Liberal reforms still in full cry, Winston was promoted to the position of Home Secretary, making him responsible for the internal affairs of England and Wales, as well as for matters related to immigration and citizenship. In addition, it was also his job to oversee matters of national security, including the police forces. His term proved to be controversial, as people all over the country began to ask uncomfortable questions regarding his responses to three major incidents: the Tonypandy Riots, the "Siege of Sidney Street", and the continuing agitation of the suffragettes who wanted to give women the vote.

He didn't last long at that post, and was soon transferred to a different office, that of the First Lord of the Admiralty. He became responsible for the command and general governance of the British naval forces of the time, and he quickly implemented various innovations. Perhaps the most important of these changes would be for the Royal Navy to switch from coal-fired engines to oil-fired ones: this would require that every seaworthy vessel be refitted with a new engine, and was also highly dependent on a steady supply of affordable oil.

With the outbreak of the First World War in 1914, the deeply divided partisan politics of the United Kingdom at the time ground to a temporary halt.

Chapter 5: World War I and Interregnum

Though Winston still needed to look after the affairs of the Royal Navy during the duration of the First World War, he was also called upon to deal with crises both domestic and international.

Beginning in late 1914, a small group of high-ranking officers in the British Army tried to persuade the government and agencies such as the War Office to look into developing armored vehicles, which could be used to break through barricades and as mobile platforms for heavy guns. However, their suggestions fell on deaf ears. It then fell to the Royal Navy to take the first steps toward that development – and in this case, the officers found an enthusiastic proponent in Winston. He formed the Landships Committee in 1915, bringing together various engineers, industrialists, and naval officers to design and build a viable prototype for what would later be called the tank.

However, Winston's political opponents called the entire idea a waste and a misuse of funds that would have been better spent on the men in the trenches. The first tank sorties seemed to bear out that criticism – the vehicles had been deployed too early, and in such small numbers so as to make their real tactical advantages difficult to take advantage of. This was the exact opposite of what Winston wanted, which was to produce a large fleet of tanks that could plow through barbed wire and other defenses, and create breakthrough sectors, particularly in areas where enemy soldiers had hunkered down in their trenches.

Despite the multiple disappointments surrounding the project, work on the tank continued, and in later years Britain and many other countries would be able to produce more powerful models that could be put to effective use on the different fronts of wartime.

Winston then set his sights on the Gallipoli peninsula in Turkey and the body of water that surrounded it, the Dardanelles. The idea was to secure the peninsula and that section of Turkey in order to open a sea route that could be used by Britain and its allies – which included Russia. If Allied powers held the Dardanelles, then the ships and armies of Russia would be able to cross more easily towards the various fronts of the war.

The problem was the Ottoman Empire: while at that time they were pejoratively known as "the sick man of Europe", they were still determined to defend their borders and expand where possible – with Germany generously sending them the military aid that they needed. Any attempt at taking Gallipoli and the Dardanelles would effectively be an invasion of a hostile power.

Winston believed that it could be done with enough men and with enough ships, and ordered several officers to make plans to land on Gallipoli.

The naval campaign commenced in mid-February 1915, when a task force comprised of British and French vessels began to fire on the Ottoman forts and artillery located along the coast overlooking the Dardanelles. While they met with initial success, they also ran into difficulties almost immediately: from bad weather to the unwelcome discovery that the Ottoman batteries were more mobile than expected. This prevented the minesweepers that were supposed to clear the Dardanelles from doing their work.

Good news came in the form of an intercepted German message, which stated that the Ottoman forts were running low on ammunition. Emboldened, the British and French vessels prepared to attack in March – and ran straight into the mines that the Ottomans had laid in the waters of the strait. Several vessels were sunk and with them, their crews, and the naval officers sounded the retreat in the face of an unacceptable loss of lives.

With the naval campaign in shambles, Winston changed tack and ordered ground forces to move in and destroy the mobile Ottoman batteries, in the hopes that clearing those weapons out would allow the ships to move into the strait unmolested. The Mediterranean Expeditionary Force, composed of British, French, Australian, and New Zealander soldiers, was tasked to carry out this mission, and were placed under the command of Ian Hamilton.

Bad weather again dogged the Allies as the date of landing on the peninsula approached – and when the skies were finally clear enough for the soldiers to make for the shore, they set out toward unfamiliar terrain and a slog toward the Ottoman positions. Only a handful of the regiments were able to land with relatively few problems; in stark contrast, soldiers at the other sites were cut down by machine-gun fire.

With the reduced Allied ground forces on one side and the limited numbers of Ottoman soldiers on the other, a four-month-long campaign of attrition began: both sides dug their trenches and attempted to run each other off the peninsula, to no avail.

With the Ottomans distracted by the Allied ground forces, the British and French ships and submarines found some success in working through the waters of the Dardanelles. It was a small consolation to Winston and the others back in England, as they continued to receive reports of men falling to failed offensives and, as the spring ground on into summer, diseases such as dysentery.

Evacuation was the only way out for the Allied soldiers; in the meantime, autumn and then winter decimated the survivors, who drowned in the trenches during rainstorms and then froze to death when the snows began to fall.

As one of the principal architects of the campaign – which was now perceived in many countries as a major disaster – Winston shouldered much of the blame that came his way from both the political establishment and the public at large. He lost the position of First Lord of the Admiralty and was demoted to the sinecure of Chancellor of the Duchy of Lancaster, but eventually resigned from the Cabinet in November of 1915, though he did not lose his seat as a member of Parliament.

January 1916 saw him being given the temporary rank of lieutenant colonel in the British Army, and he went to the Western Front to command the 6th Battalion of the Royal Scots Fusiliers. He experienced the horrors and difficulties of trench warfare at first hand, and accompanied his men on several sorties into no man's land.

He was brought back into the Cabinet in 1917 when he was appointed as Minister for Munitions, and then he took the posts of Secretary of State for War and Secretary of State for Air. While he was able to win some concessions, he was stymied on many of his pet causes and initiatives, and he eventually lost even his position in the House of Commons during the 1922 general election – he had become ill during the campaign and had to have his appendix taken out, so he couldn't campaign as effectively as he had in other elections. Winston was able to reenter public life and politics in 1924; he became a member of Parliament for Epping, rejoined the Conservatives, and was appointed to the position of Chancellor of the Exchequer, overseeing all matters related to economics and finance. But he made another great mistake by pressing for a return to the Gold Standard; this resulted in widespread unemployment, deflation, and eventually a general strike in 1926.

He became estranged once again from the leadership of the Conservative Party, and during what he called "the wilderness years" distracted himself through writing and painting. He gave speeches denouncing the movement towards Indian independence, and spoke out against Germany's attempts to rebuild its armed forces – but at the same time, he praised Benito Mussolini's fascist ideas.

Chapter 6: World War II

After 1936 and the German takeover of the Rhineland, Winston tried to convince the British government and public that they needed to push back against German rearmament and the military aggression of the Nazi Party. He strongly criticized then-Prime Minister Neville Chamberlain's efforts to appease Adolf Hitler, and wrote to other politicians in the hopes of convincing them to add their voices to his. Britain finally declared war on Nazi Germany in 1939, and Winston was once again appointed to the position of First Lord of the Admiralty – which was the same position that he held in World War I. This meant that he would again oversee the operations of the Royal Navy, no trivial task considering that at the time it was the largest navy in the world. Reinforcements even joined up right at the outbreak of war: three destroyers and two submarines from the Polish Navy. During the "Phoney War" phase of the conflict, Winston suggested to the War Cabinet that Britain should move ahead of Germany, and take over several ports and mines in Norway and in Sweden in order to secure their supplies of iron. He was voted down, and those supplies were lost after Germany invaded Norway – but the disappointment that this failure engendered in both the government and in the public led straight to the removal of Chamberlain as Prime Minister. Winston was not the first choice for the job – that honor belonged to Lord Halifax – but despite lingering resentment and lack of popularity, he immediately threw himself straight into the work that needed to be done. He adamantly refused to consider any ideas of armistice, and declared that Britain would continue to fight, even if it would have to fight all by itself. This encouraged the idea of resistance in the countries comprising the British Empire, and more importantly allowed Britain to become the foundation and springboard for the Allied advance from 1942 to the war's end.

In private, Winston did not flinch back from the general sentiment that they were fighting a hopeless war, even going so far as to tell his chief military assistant Hastings Ismay that they were probably going to die within the next three months. In public, however, he showed that he was willing to do whatever it might take in order to fight back, and to keep on fighting in the face of hopeless odds. He created the Cabinet-level position of Minister of Defence and then took it for himself, at once quelling criticism that in previous conflicts there had been no single person in charge of all wartime decision-making, and making himself the most powerful wartime Prime Minister in British history.

He had the gift of seeing – and in many cases, foreseeing – what his country would be needing in the years and conflicts to come.

He placed his friend, the industrialist Lord Beaverbrook, in charge of aircraft production; this made it possible to streamline and speed up the many processes of design, engineering, and production involved in building the various aircraft that would be vital in turning the tide of the war.

He was a key player in the formation of what would eventually become known as Special Operations Executive, an organization of spies, saboteurs, and reconnaissance agents. Their main tasks were twofold: to conduct covert warfare operations against the Axis powers, and to give whatever assistance they could to the many resistance organizations scattered all over the world. The few people who knew of the organization's very existence referred to its members as "the Baker Street Irregulars" or as "the Ministry of Ungentlemanly Warfare" -- and Winston's influence on the group was made clear by the nickname "Churchill's Secret Army". SOE became one of the templates on which the American Office of Strategic Services would be built. (OSS later became one of the ancestors of the modern Central Intelligence Agency.)

He was also one of the key movers behind the formation of a military force that would be tasked with carrying out special operations against the enemy. He wanted soldiers who would be capable of working behind enemy lines, and who would fight as the very tip of the spear. The British Commandos carried out all kinds of raids over the course of the war, and were ultimately the ancestor unit of the Royal Marine Commandos, Special Air Service, Special Boat Service, as well as of similar units in Europe and the United States (specifically, the 1st Battalion of the US Army Rangers).

It might be a surprise to think that by the time he was made Prime Minister, Winston was already 65 years old. The sentiment was summed up in a 1941 comment from an American journalist:

"The responsibilities which are his now must be greater than those carried by any other human being on earth. One would think such a weight would have a crushing effect upon him. Not at all. The last time I saw him, while the Battle of Britain was still raging, he looked twenty years younger than before the war began [...]"

Not only did Winston look twenty years younger even as the Second World War dragged on – he carried on working with what seemed like the strength of twenty men, so much so that he would dismiss his younger aides and even officers in the armed forces to their rest and keep on working himself, often well past midnight.

He would not have been without his share of sleepless nights, especially during the first few years of the war. It would have been easy to understand if he felt that Nazi Germany had drawn a great big bull's-eye on his country, what with the double whammy of the Battle of Britain, and then the Blitz. Adolf Hitler had long been laying plans for an amphibious and airborne invasion of Britain; a major part of what would become known as Operation Sea Lion was using the bombers and fighters of the Luftwaffe (the German Air Force) in order to soften the country up, as well as destroy overall morale. But Winston and the Royal Air Force turned out to be more than capable of fighting – or in this case, dogfighting – a seemingly unstoppable enemy head-on. Winston had taken flying lessons himself, and had long been an advocate of using various fighter aircraft in battle. It was no wonder that he threw his whole-hearted support to the RAF – even to the point of making hard and potentially unpopular decisions.

Despite bombing damage to aircraft production facilities and an initial shortage of trained and experienced fighter pilots, the RAF were able to make good use of every resource available: from radar to German intelligence intercepts to the new ideas of individual soldiers.

Much is made of the bravery and persistence of the RAF pilots flying defensive sorties in the very skies of their own country, but Winston also knew that there were British bombers conducting night-time raids over cities in Germany and occupied France – and by striking at military installations, logistical targets, and barges that had been prepared to cross the English Channel, the invasion of Britain was postponed time and time again.

But that did not mean that Winston, or Britain for that matter, could take a moment to rest. Barely two months into the Battle of Britain, German intelligence came to the erroneous conclusion that the RAF were down to its last reserves, and should therefore be drawn out to be annihilated. Thus commenced a campaign of heavy air raids targeting the major cities of the United Kingdom, including London, the capital; important ports such as Liverpool, Bristol, and Plymouth; and industrial cities such as Coventry, Glasgow, and Manchester.

London took the brunt of both infrastructure damage and human losses, but it must have been a source of hope and strength to the citizens of that war-torn city that neither the Royal Family nor the Prime Minister and his War Cabinet were willing to evacuate to safety.

Knowing that the citizens of the country needed that same hope and strength, Winston made the time to travel all around the United Kingdom for the express purpose of raising morale. It didn't matter if he was going to a bombed-out city or to a seemingly idyllic farm. It didn't matter if he was seeing women who were once again bereft of their sons and brothers and husbands, or the elderly who had hoped that the First World War would not be repeated in their lifetimes, or the children who were beginning to flinch away from the sounds of air-raid sirens. He looked them all in the eyes and gave them reassurance – but at the same time he told them the hard truths that they needed to hear. He told them to hunker down and he told them to do everything in their power to support their soldiers.

As for those soldiers – he didn't forget them as he didn't forget the pilots. It could even be argued that he couldn't forget them, since he had already lived through one great global conflict and was now up to his shoulders in another. He visited the soldiers and inquired after their needs. Numerous photographs show Winston surrounded by the officers and the enlisted alike, firing their weapons and sharing a smoke or two. He didn't just go to the bases, either – he went to the battlefields, too, when it was safe for him to rub shoulders with the men.

There were, of course, many other official trips to be made: Winston established both diplomatic ties and a personal friendship with then-US president Franklin D. Roosevelt, as well as a somewhat more reluctant relationship with Joseph Stalin of the USSR. In Tehran, Yalta, and, for a short while, Potsdam, the three leaders tried to work out what would happen to Europe as a whole at war's end. These three conferences, however, also marked the transition from the open warfare that had characterized both the First and Second World Wars, to the diplomatic maneuvering and covert actions that would become a hallmark of what would become known as the Cold War.

Chapter 7: Great Speeches

The greatest thing that Winston ever did for his country – and, by extension, the world that was listening avidly to him on the radio – was deliver a series of fiery, impassioned speeches during the Second World War. No cut-and-dried recitations of facts, these. He had to deliver a lot of bad news during the first years of the war; he had to wait a few years before he could start adding honest-to-goodness great news. Still, he told the truth without flinching, every single time.

More importantly, however, he always made it clear that despite the bad news he sincerely and strongly believed in the hope of eventual victory.

And more often than not, his words would have the intended effect: he buoyed up his people's spirits and gave them tremendous courage for the difficult days ahead.

Winston had a lot of speeches to deliver in 1940, the year he was appointed to the position of Prime Minister – but this was also the year in which the German war machine seemed to roll unopposed through much of Europe. The enormous burden of reporting the bad news was placed on his shoulders.

Appropriately enough for someone who was as skilled in the use and delivery of the English language as he was, his very first speech made an electrifying initial impression indeed. Often referred to as the "Blood, toil, tears, and sweat" speech, he delivered it to the House of Commons on the 13th of May, three days after becoming Prime Minister. Through this speech, he was asking the members of Parliament to declare their confidence in the government that he was forming.

"To form an Administration of this scale and complexity is a serious undertaking in itself, but it must be remembered that we are in the preliminary stage of one of the greatest battles in history, that we are in action at many other points in Norway and in Holland, that we have to be prepared in the Mediterranean, that the air battle is continuous and that many preparations, such as have been indicated by my honorable friend below the gangway, have to be made here at home. In this crisis I hope I may be pardoned if I do not address the House at any length today. I hope that any of my friends and colleagues, or former colleagues, who are affected by the political reconstruction, will make allowance, all allowance, for any lack of ceremony with which it has been necessary to act. I would say to the House, as I said to those who have joined this government: 'I have nothing to offer but blood, toil, tears and sweat.'

"We have before us an ordeal of the most grievous kind. We have before us many, many long months of struggle and of suffering. You ask, what is our policy? I can say: It is to wage war, by sea, land and air, with all our might and with all the strength that God can give us; to wage war against a monstrous tyranny, never surpassed in the dark, lamentable catalogue of human crime. That is our policy. You ask, what is our aim? I can answer in one word: It is victory, victory at all costs, victory in spite of all terror, victory, however long and hard the road may be; for without victory, there is no survival. [...]"

The motion of confidence that Winston had asked for passed unanimously, and it seemed that the heckling and distrust of "the wilderness years" had been swept away, now that he had been revealed to be the right man for the dangerous and difficult task of leading Britain through the Second World War.

But this speech was delivered only to one group of lawmakers. The rest of the country, at the time, had no idea what Winston would do, with war literally knocking on their very doors and windows.

In his first address to the country as Prime Minister, Winston had to tell his countrymen that the Germans had invaded France, and that the British armed forces were scrambling to assist their allies. He had to tell them that the Netherlands had already been defeated, and that there was a very real possibility that Germany would attempt to invade Britain. And he talked about his, and the country's, ultimate goal:

"Our task is not only to win the battle – but to win the War. After this battle in France abates its force, there will come the battle for our island – for all that Britain is, and all that Britain means – that will be the struggle. In that supreme emergency we shall not hesitate to take every step, even the most drastic, to call forth from our people, the last ounce and the last inch of effort they are capable."

This speech is referred to as the Be ye men of valour speech for its closing paragraph, where Winston quotes the First Book of Maccabees:

"Today is Trinity Sunday. Centuries ago words were written to be a call and a spur to the faithful servants of Truth and Justice: 'Arm yourselves, and be ye men of valour, and be in readiness for the conflict; for it is better for us to perish in battle than to look upon the outrage of our nation and our altar. As the Will of God is in Heaven, even so let it be.'"

The Battle of France ended with the defeat of the French armed forces – but the British could only think of a miraculous deliverance, since the evacuation from Dunkirk had been so wildly and unexpectedly successful. It was easy to understand why the mood in the nation was one of relief – but Winston, as always, saw it as his task to be clear-eyed and levelheaded, and that was the main emotion that he conveyed in his speech of June 4, 1940, the "We shall fight on the beaches" speech: "Even though large tracts of Europe and many old and famous States have fallen or may fall into the grip of the Gestapo and all the odious apparatus of Nazi rule, we shall not flag or fail. We shall go on to the end. We shall fight in France, we shall fight on the seas and oceans, we shall fight with growing confidence and growing strength in the air, we shall defend our island, whatever the cost may be. We shall fight on the beaches, we shall fight on the landing grounds, we shall fight in the fields and in the streets, we shall fight in the hills; we shall never surrender, and if, which I do not for a moment believe, this island or a large part of it were subjugated and starving, then our Empire beyond the seas, armed and guarded by the British Fleet, would carry on the struggle, until, in God's good time, the New World, with all its power and might, steps forth to the rescue and the liberation of the old." The final part of the speech moved listeners to tears. France signed an armistice with Germany on June 16, and Winston and the rest of the government had no choice but to consider that Britain was next on Hitler's list – so in a speech delivered on June 18, Winston spoke of the readiness of the British armed forces, closing with: "What General Weygand called the Battle of France is over. I expect that the Battle of Britain is about to begin. Upon this battle depends the survival of Christian civilization. Upon it depends our own British life, and the long continuity of our institutions and our Empire. The whole fury and might of the enemy must very soon be turned on us. Hitler knows that he will have to break us in this Island or lose the war. If we can stand up to him, all Europe may be free and the life of the world may move forward into broad, sunlit uplands. But if we fail, then the whole world, including the United States, including all that we have known and cared for, will sink into the abyss of a new Dark Age made more sinister, and perhaps more protracted, by the lights of perverted science. Let us therefore brace ourselves to our duties, and so bear ourselves that, if the British Empire and its Commonwealth last for a thousand years, men will still say, 'This was their finest hour.'"

Within a month, Germany had fired the opening salvos of the very same Battle of Britain that Winston had predicted. In response, the RAF jumped into action despite still being widely perceived as an untested fighting force, while the Royal Navy placed itself as a blockade to protect its own home shores. Winston made his support and admiration of the pilots, their support crews, and their commanders clear in his speech of August 20:

"But all depends now upon the whole life-strength of the British race in every part of the world and of all our associated peoples and of all our well-wishers in every land, doing their utmost night and day, giving all, daring all, enduring all-to the utmost-to the end. This is no war of chieftains or of princes, of dynasties or national ambition; it is a war of peoples and of causes. There are vast numbers, not only in this Island but in every land, who will render faithful service in this war, but whose names will never be known, whose deeds will never be recorded. This is a War of the Unknown Warriors; but let all strive without failing in faith or in duty, and the dark curse of Hitler will be lifted from our age."

As the fighters and bombers struck relentlessly at each other in the British skies, Winston saluted the RAF, and tried to reassure his people that despite the many defeats suffered by their side in the war, things would soon be turning a corner.

"The gratitude of every home in our Island, in our Empire, and indeed throughout the world, except in the abodes of the guilty, goes out to the British airmen who, undaunted by odds, unwearied in their constant challenge and mortal danger, are turning the tide of the world war by their prowess and by their devotion. Never in the field of human conflict was so much owed by so many to so few."

He was actually already telling them the truth without being aware of it, which is only understandable; after all, with pilots fighting for their very lives in the skies overhead, he couldn't have known that the Battle of Britain would result in a British victory – and yet the speech talks about just that hope that they would prevail.

The RAF has since adopted with great pride the nickname that Winston coined for them, "the Few".

Winston's 1940 speeches may have gotten his entire country, and indeed much of the world that was listening in, through that long and painful year – but such was his genius that he could still be counted on to coin a meaningful phrase or two as the tide began to turn in the Allies' favor.

Given the opportunity in 1941 to return to Harrow to sing the songs that he remembered from his school days, he was treated to a heartfelt rendition of "Stet Fortuna Domus" with an entirely new final verse, dedicated to him. In turn, he kindled hope and determination in his listeners with an equally sincere exhortation:

"You cannot tell from appearances how things will go. Sometimes imagination makes things out far worse than they are; yet without imagination not much can be done. Those people who are imaginative see many more dangers than perhaps exist; certainly many more than will happen; but then they must also pray to be given that extra courage to carry this far-reaching imagination. But for everyone, surely, what we have gone through in this period – I am addressing myself to the school – surely from this period of ten months this is the lesson: never give in, never give in, never, never, never – in nothing, great or small, large or petty – never give in except to convictions of honor and good sense. Never yield to force; never yield to the apparently overwhelming might of the enemy. We stood all alone a year ago, and to many countries it seemed that our account was closed, we were finished. [...]"

There was good news to be heard all throughout the next year, with success and victory being found on several fronts – and Winston surely rejoiced, as did those around him. Still, it didn't stop him from advising caution, and from reminding his friends and countrymen that there were still many battles left to be fought and won. In 1942, soon after hearing about Allied victories in North Africa, he said:

"This is not the end. It is not even the beginning of the end. But it is, perhaps, the end of the beginning."

Fittingly, this chapter ends with the powerful, simple speech that Winston delivered on V-E Day, May 8, 1945. With this speech, he captured Britain's struggle and its ultimate reward – and with its response to the beginning of the speech, the London crowds roared back their thanks to the man who had helped them get through that struggle.

"My dear friends, this is your hour. [The people cried, "No, it's yours!" in response.] This is not victory of a party or of any class. It is a victory of the great British nation as a whole. We were the first, in this ancient island, to draw the sword against tyranny. After a while we were left all alone against the most tremendous military power that has been seen. We were all alone for a whole year.

"There we stood, alone. Did anyone want to give in? ["No," cried the crowd.] Were we down-hearted? ["No!"] The lights went out and the bombs came down. But every man, woman, and child in the country had no thought of quitting the struggle. London can take it. So we came back after long months from the jaws of death, out of the mouth of hell, while all the world wondered. When shall the reputation and faith of this generation of English men and women fail? I say that in the long years to come not only will the people of this island but of the world, wherever the bird of freedom chirps in human hearts, look back to what we have done, and they will say 'Do not despair, do not yield to violence and tyranny, march straightforward and die if need be – unconquered.' Now we have emerged from one deadly struggle – a terrible foe has been cast on the ground and awaits our judgment and our mercy. [...]"

Chapter 8: Overcoming Great Difficulties

History has made much of the observation that during the Second World War, Winston found himself in precisely the right place and the right time to become a hero – not only in his own country, but to everyone who sympathized with the Allied powers. But what happened to him after the war? Winston resigned from the position of Prime Minister at the end of the war, and after general elections were held, eventually became the Leader of the Opposition in the House of Commons. He still had many opportunities to change the world for what he felt was the better: he spoke out against the formation of the Eastern Bloc and the looming threat of communism. Instead, he promoted the idea of pan-European cooperation – in his own words, something like a "United States of Europe". By speaking in favor of European unity, it could be considered that he was one of the driving forces behind the eventual formation of the Council of Europe, which promotes democracy, human rights, and the rule of law in its member states.

He was once again to serve as Prime Minister from 1951 to 1955. As he had done near the beginning of his political career, he campaigned in support of initiatives that would benefit various sectors of society, such as protecting the health and welfare of young people and women who were working in mines, through the legislative process. He also fought to provide more housing for the country's population, which had not only been increased by the return of its soldiers from the war, but was also undergoing a boom in general. He worked to maintain Britain's special relationship with the United States, trying to forge stronger ties with Harry Truman and then with Dwight Eisenhower to do so.

But the ravages of time and his advancing age began to take their inevitable toll on him as his second term wore on. From 1949 to 1963 he suffered from a total of ten strokes, each dealing its own damage to his once-formidable mental faculties. While in many cases he could still be the consummate politician and speaker, as the years went on he began to need more and more help to present that formidable facade to the world – and he also began to depend more and more heavily on alcohol and tobacco to get him through the intense days.

Some things, however, not even alcohol or tobacco could cure.

There is no doubt that a large part of the isolation that Winston felt most keenly during his school years could be directly attributed to the speech impediment that he was never really able to conquer. It might be surprising to think of him as suffering from a lisp, but he did: he had a real difficulty with pronouncing his S sounds.

So how, then, was he able to deliver his powerful speeches? How was he able to express himself so grandly and eloquently? In his case, the adage "practice makes perfect" would have certainly played a large role: even as he drafted a speech and worked on developing its themes, he would have taken the time to practice delivering the speech itself. That advice, backed up by a recommendation from a prominent speech therapist in the 1890s to work on his pronunciation, made it possible for him to gain his reputation for powerful rhetoric. He also had some more prosaic ways of getting around the problem, such as getting dentures that were especially designed to help him minimize his lisp.

He even turned some of his memorable mispronunciations into points of interest in his speeches, as when he memorably insisted on saying "Narzees" instead of properly saying "Nazis"; this way he could make use of the name in many different ways. With the right intonation and the right facial expressions, he could turn that word into a grotesque joke that turned the enemy into a laughingstock, or into a scathing insult designed to belittle and demoralize them.

So the issue of Winston having a lisp and not, as some chroniclers have erroneously suggested, a stammer has been laid to rest by history.

What of the controversy regarding his mental health?

Much of the brouhaha over Winston's struggle with "the Black Dog" of depression comes from what was thought to be a reliable first-hand source: the alleged diaries of Winston's physician, Lord Moran. The diaries claimed that Winston suffered from despair and from recurring severe depression, and those claims seemed to be backed up by later information taken from the biographies of Winston's close associates. However, new historical research has revealed that Lord Moran did not actually keep any diaries during his years as Winston's doctor; the information in the so-called source material was actually little more than an arbitrary mish-mash of case notes and material that did not come from Lord Moran himself.

In his own letters and writings, Winston mentioned "the Black Dog" just once, when he wrote to his wife, Clementine, about his interest in a relative's complete and successful recovery from depression.

On the other hand, Winston spoke more or less openly about the general ebb and flow of his emotions and mental health in his book Painting as a Pastime, in which he explained that he often suffered from the cumulative effects of worry, anxiety, and "mental overstrain" as an entirely understandable result of having to carry the weight of the responsibilities that he did in the course of his life.

Perhaps it would be more prudent to look, instead, at the case notes of the neurologist W. Russell Brain. He first saw Winston after the 1949 stroke, and continued to work with him until shortly before his death. Brain noted that perhaps Winston might have been subject to mild mood swings, but could not be in any way described as suffering from any form of depression.

If we understand that it was the very nature of Winston's work and responsibilities that caused him to feel, at times, anxiety, worry, and piercing but temporary sadness, then we can understand that in many ways he had already found the remedies for the burdens that weighed him down. He could find solace in his family, and especially in his wife. He could lose himself in the prosaic task of laying bricks – and he was such a good "brickie" that he could put together such different structures as a swimming pool, a goldfish pond, and a garden wall. He could distract himself from the problems of his country and of his people by taking an uncommon interest in the welfare and doings of the animals on the family farm, Chartwell, and in breeding racehorses.

Perhaps the pastime that allowed him to relax and temporarily shrug off the cares of the world the most was art. He took up painting after leaving public life in the wake of the disaster at Gallipolli, and his teachers later on commented that he had a well-developed understanding of how light and color might affect a subject for painting, and in turn be affected by that same subject. Two of his paintings were even accepted by the Royal Academy of Arts, though he submitted them under the pseudonym "David Winter" so as not to exert any unnecessary influence on the leadership of that institution.

Chapter 9: Churchill's 10 Rules for Success

Courage Comes First

Describe Winston Churchill in one word, what comes to mind? For many, courageous would be the first response. A trait required by most leaders, he produced courage through all stages of his career. At one such time during the 1930's, many considered his political career all but over. It was at this time he was one of the only voices warning the rise of Hitler and his Nazi party. It was an unpopular opinion with few fellow comrades wanting to face the harsh truth. Did this shut him up? I think you know the answer. Everything Churchill accomplished in his life arose from a root of courage.

'COURAGE IS RIGHTLY ESTEEMED THE FIRST OF HUMAN QUALITIES... BECAUSE IT IS THE QUALITY WHICH GUARANTEES ALL OTHERS.'

– WINSTON CHURCHILL

Master The Written Word

Churchill's early encounters with education were mainly below average. Nonetheless, it became apparent when his interests and passions were roused, he had the gift of writing and memorization. Of all the skills and traits he possessed, above all, he was a writer. He would hand write his speeches, believing the written word a great tool for inspiration and leadership. Through exposure to great English writers, he self educated and formed his own recognizable writing style. He also wrote a number of history books including his own Six Volume Account of World War II.

'WRITING A BOOK IS AN ADVENTURE. TO BEGIN WITH IT IS A TOY AND AN AMUSEMENT. THEN IT BECOMES A MISTRESS, THEN IT BECOMES A MASTER, THEN IT BECOMES A TYRANT. THE LAST PHASE IS THAT JUST AS YOU ARE ABOUT TO BE RECONCILED TO YOUR SERVITUDE, YOU KILL THE MONSTER AND FLING HIM TO THE PUBLIC.'

–WINSTON CHURCHILL

Master The Spoken Word

Although initially a writer, it is as a speaker Churchill is predominately remembered. To quote President Kennedy, Churchill 'mobilized the English language and sent it into battle'. During Britain's darkest hours, with anxious families huddled around their radio, Churchill would deliver masterfully crafted speeches with a voice full of unshakeable confidence and grit. The result, a boost in morale and general confidence throughout that Britain was in good hands. Considering Churchill started life with a lisp, his oratory achievements are all the more impressive. It should be noted that this skill did not come naturally to Churchill. He would prepare extensively, speaking to audiences with methodically crafted ideas and very little impromptu.

'IT WAS MY AMBITION, ALL MY LIFE, TO BE A MASTER OF THE SPOKEN WORD. THAT WAS MY ONLY AMBITION.'

–WINSTON CHURCHILL

'OF ALL THE TALENTS BESTOWED UPON MEN, NONE IS SO PRECIOUS AS THE GIFT OF ORATORY. HE WHO ENJOYS IT WIELDS A POWER MORE DURABLE THAN THAT OF A GREAT KING. HE IS AN INDEPENDENT FORCE IN THE WORLD. ABANDONED BY HIS PARTY, BETRAYED BY HIS FRIENDS, STRIPPED OF HIS OFFICES, WHOEVER CAN COMMAND THIS POWER IS STILL FORMIDABLE.'

–WINSTON CHURCHILL

Loyalty And Love

Churchill loved his country, his monarch and the British Empire. He had this love his entire life, which provided the energy and enthusiasm to lead and serve up until the day he died. It was this love that provided the inspiration to perform great speeches, write great books, paint great pictures and lead his country through thick and thin. Not forgetting his love and loyalty to his wife, Clementine. They were married until his death.

'MY MOST BRILLIANT ACHIEVEMENT WAS MY ABILITY TO BE
ABLE TO PERSUADE MY WIFE TO MARRY ME.'

-WINSTON CHURCHILL

Complete Self Confidence

Born to the aristocracy at Blenheim Palace, Churchill was definitely not a 'self made man'. It would be fair to refer to him though, as 'self created'. He thought extremely highly of himself and that he and his life were destined for greatness. He thought this despite his numerous limitations- from a distracting speech impediment to a very limited physical appearance and performance. This unyielding belief in himself would guide him through every decision, setback and action in life. Churchill was continually evolving and never satisfied, the process of self-creation never ending. This ensured his recovery from all of his many setbacks that would have been the end of a lesser man.

'HISTORY WILL BE KIND TO ME FOR I INTEND TO WRITE IT.'

-WINSTON CHURCHILL

Live With Unconquerable Grit As A Way To Lead By Example

There can be no doubt that Churchill was not short of grit. Defined as: courage and resolve; strength of character. This is a trait each person is entirely self responsible for, further adding to the argument of Churchill's self-creation. Relying majorly on continuous effort, not strength and intelligence. Such a trait is infectious, and once seen in action can't help but inspire those witnessing it. His journey was filled with examples of determination against all odds, occasionally against expert opinion, always staying true to oneself.

'CONTINUOUS EFFORT—NOT STRENGTH OR INTELLIGENCE—
IS THE KEY TO UNLOCKING OUR POTENTIAL.'

–WINSTON CHURCHILL

Live as an Artist

A great deal of men dismiss arts and crafts as a useless, feminine hobby. Not Churchill. More so later in life, he became an avid painter. This activity helped ease any bouts of depression he faced, referring to the illness as the 'Black Dog'. His paintings are still popular throughout the art world and very sought over. As you may know Hitler's first career choice was to become an artist. Although I'm sure the popular opinion will be biased, it is argued by most that Churchill's paintings are of a higher quality. Upping his old rival once again. It is not only through his paintings that Churchill lived as an artist. He strode the world stage as a true leader putting on a performance for all to see.

'PAINTING IS A COMPANION WITH WHOM ONE MAY WALK A GREAT PART OF LIFE'S JOURNEY.'

-WINSTON CHURCHILL

Insight is Superior to Intellect

Churchill was forever curious and largely self directed. This allowed him to see past the limits of conventional wisdom and look at situations from another angle. Through a variety of wordly experiences he became obviously gifted with insight. Combine this with his temperament and it would be quite the common occurrence for him to express his often unexpected points of view. Judgement is a good thing, but not all that uncommon. Deep insight is much rarer. Churchill has moments of that deep insight, brought forth through his outspoken nature.

'WHEN HITLER CAME TO POWER CHURCHILL DID NOT USE JUDGMENT BUT ONE OF HIS DEEP INSIGHTS. THIS WAS ABSOLUTE DANGER, THERE WAS NO EASY WAY ROUND. THAT WAS WHAT WE NEEDED. IT WAS A UNIQUE OCCASION IN OUR HISTORY. IT HAD TO BE GRASPED BY A NATIONALIST LEADER. PLENTY OF PEOPLE ON THE LEFT COULD SEE THE DANGER: BUT THEY DID NOT KNOW HOW THE COUNTRY HAD TO BE SEIZED AND UNIFIED.'

–C.P. SNOW

Perseverance

In my opinion, the one particular trait above all others that epitomizes Churchill as a man would have to be perseverance. Churchill never gave up. Whether that was defending his country, battling his own political party or simply mastering a painting, he was not a quitter. Idleness was to be avoided at all costs. After 6 long years, the Nazis finally surrendered 8th May 1945. Only 2 months later, Churchill lost the general election, rejected by the very people he had led to victory. I'm sure at this point many a man would, understandably, react with anger and bitterness whilst throwing in the towel. Churchill however, stayed on as leader of his political party and in 1950 led his party to victory once more, reinstating himself as Prime Minister.

'NEVER GIVE IN. NEVER GIVE IN. NEVER, NEVER, NEVER, NEVER -- IN NOTHING, GREAT OR SMALL, LARGE OR PETTY -- NEVER GIVE IN, EXCEPT TO CONVICTIONS OF HONOR AND GOOD SENSE.'

-WINSTON CHURCHILL

Willingness to Fight

'WE SHALL GO ON TO THE END. WE SHALL FIGHT IN FRANCE,
WE SHALL FIGHT ON THE SEAS AND OCEANS, WE SHALL
FIGHT WITH GROWING CONFIDENCE AND GROWING
STRENGTH IN THE AIR, WE SHALL DEFEND OUR ISLAND,
WHATEVER THE COST MAY BE. WE SHALL FIGHT ON THE
BEACHES, WE SHALL FIGHT ON THE LANDING GROUNDS, WE
SHALL FIGHT IN THE FIELDS AND IN THE STREETS, WE SHALL
FIGHT IN THE HILLS; WE SHALL NEVER SURRENDER.'

-WINSTON CHURCHILL

Chapter 10: Little Known Facts

Love for cigars

During the Cuban war of independence in 1895, Churchill travelled to Cuba working for the Daily Graphic to write about the conflict between the Spanish and the insurgent Cuban Guerillas. On his twenty-first birthday he came under fire for the first time in his life. This would happen on approximately 50 more occasions over the years. Churchill enjoyed his time in Cuba and was also awarded his first medal. It would be the Havana Cigars that left the longest impression though, which he soon acquired a taste for and would smoke for the rest of his life.

Accident-prone

Whilst playfully throwing himself off a bridge as a youth, Churchill ruptured a kidney and suffered a concussion. Continuing this trend throughout life he fell from numerous horses, nearly drowned in a Swiss lake, crashed a plane whilst learning to fly, dislocated his shoulder when exiting a ship in India and was hit by a car when crossing the road on New York's famous Fifth Avenue. Although often knocked down, he would always rise living to the ripe old of age of 90 before finally suffering a fatal stroke.

Operation Unthinkable

Almost before World War 2 had ended Churchill was drawing up plans that would undoubtedly start World War 3. Named "Operation Unthinkable" for good reason, the plans called for a surprise attack against the then-allied Soviet Union and included rearming up to 100,000 former Nazi soldiers. This plan became the first Cold War era contingency plan for a potential war with the Soviet Union. At the time these plans were top secret and it was not until 1998 that this information was released to the general public.

Love of Alcohol

Whilst Winston was the epitome of a British bulldog in both appearance and temperament, when it came to alcohol he had more continental tastes and a large appetite. Whilst his love of alcohol may be quite well known, the extent to which he drank is not.

"I drink champagne at all meals, and buckets of claret and soda in between," he was not ashamed of saying. He also stated "Hot baths, cold champagne, new peas and old brandy" were the four essentials of life. During the ferocious struggle with the Nazis, a royal visitor reported that Winston was putting away enough champagne to "undermine the health of any ordinary man."

Thankfully for the British people, Churchill was no ordinary man.

This wasn't anything new; at the beginning of his career Churchill took 60 bottles of booze with him when he set out for the Boer War. During his 1941 visit to the White House he, of course, spent much of his personal time naked and drinking brandy

It would be unfair to say he ignored what the British Empire had to offer. Long workdays would be occupied with Scotch and sodas and the now famous Churchill martini.

"There is always some alcohol in his bloodstream," biographer William Manchester attested, "and it reaches its peak late in the evening after he has had two or three Scotches, several glasses of Champagne, at least two brandies, and a highball." To put a finer point to it, Churchill's favorite brandy was Hine, his preferred Champagne Pol Roger, and his top Scotch Johnnie Walker Red Label.

During a visit to King Ibn Saud of Saudi Arabia, for a banquet thrown in his honor. Churchill was informed he was not allowed to drink or smoke for religious purposes. Churchill did not like this idea, stating to the monarch that, "My religion prescribed as an absolute sacred ritual smoking cigars and drinking alcohol before, after and if need be during all meals and the intervals between them."

Broken beer bottles

During the booming applause following his famous 'We shall fight on the beaches' speech to the House of Commons in 1940, rumor has it Churchill whispered to a colleague, "And we'll fight them with the butt ends of broken beer bottles because that's bloody well all we've got!"

First Honorary US citizen

In 1963 Churchill became the first honorary citizen on the United States awarded to him by then U.S President John F. Kennedy who was acting under authorization granted by an Act of Congress. Unfortunately Churchill was unable to collect the award personally so his Son and Grandson received the award on his behalf.

Iconic Image

Potentially Churchill's most iconic photo, the photograph of the cover of this book was achieved by photographer Yousef Karsh taking the ever present cigar from Churchill's mouth and immediately taking the photo of a now grumpy Churchill.

Inventor of O.M.G

In 1917 Winston received a letter from Lord Fisher in reference to the war currently being fought. Near the end of the letter Lord Fisher writes "I hear that a new order of knighthood is on the tapis-O.M.G. (Oh! My God!) – Shower it on the Admiralty."

This is the first known instance of this phrase being used and Churchill was the receiver.

Pop Charts

Making it to No. 4 on the UK album charts in 2010, The Central Band of the Royal Air Force released an album named "Reach for the Skies." Two songs from this album combined audio from some of Churchill's speeches and music from the Central Band.

From a Nobel Prize in literature, to pop charts, to artist, Winston Churchill has contributed more to society than just his famed political career. As he once said, "History will be kind to me for I intend to write it." And he did, and it is.

Conclusion

The ultimate question to ask when judging a person's mark on history is: would events have turned out differently but for their service? With Churchill this is a resounding yes. The history of England, Europe and even the history of the world would have taken a different turn especially during the years 1940-41 had Churchill not contributed his services to the cause.

This is not to say he was without his flaws, his role in WW1 was seen as a failure to many and his short temper could often flare up causing him to make rash decisions. Churchill's shortcomings only made him human, his legacy as one of the most influential people of recent history is set in stone.

If you enjoyed this book, please take the time to leave me a review on Amazon. I appreciate your honest feedback, and it really helps me to continue producing high quality books.

Printed in Great Britain
by Amazon